Contradance

to Virginia

John Peck
4 March 2019

JOHN PECK

Contradance

THE UNIVERSITY OF CHICAGO PRESS

Chicago & London

JOHN PECK is a freelance editor and translator and a practicing
Jungian analyst. He is the author of eight books of poems, most
recently of *Red Strawberry Leaf: Selected Poems, 1994–2001*, published
in the Phoenix Poets series by the University of Chicago Press, and a
cotranslator of C. G. Jung's *The Red Book*.

The University of Chicago Press, Chicago 60637
The University of Chicago Press, Ltd., London
© 2011 by The University of Chicago
All rights reserved. Published 2011.
Printed in the United States of America
20 19 18 17 16 15 14 13 12 11   1 2 3 4 5

ISBN-13: 978-0-226-65292-4 (paper)
ISBN-10: 0-226-65292-0 (paper)

Library of Congress Cataloging-in-Publication Data
Peck, John, 1941–
   Contradance / John Peck.
     p. cm. — (Phoenix poets)
   ISBN-13: 978-0-226-65292-4 (pbk. : alk. paper)
   ISBN-10: 0-226-65292-0 (pbk. : alk. paper)
   I. Title. II. Series: Phoenix poets.
   PS3566.E247C65 2011
   811'.54—dc22   2011001608

CONTENTS

ACKNOWLEDGMENTS

My gratitude to the following editors at these publications for first publishing the following poems:

Robert Archambeau, *Samizdat*: "Dawn Renga," "*Out of strife, peace,*" "*Venice's last*"

Joshua Kotin, *Chicago Review*: "Book of the Dead? We Have No Book of the Dead"

John Matthias, *Notre Dame Review*: "New York Sonnets" ("Philosophia, East 65th Street"; "The Project"; "The Web in Central Park"; "Anfiteatro Flaviano"; "The Chrysler Building, Met Life, Trump Tower"), "Violin," "1618," "Incomings"

Vern Miller and Michael Anania (guest editor), *Fifth Wednesday Journal*: "New York Sonnets" ("I Hear You Calling")

Dana Norris and Reginald Gibbons (advisory editor), *TriQuarterly*: "Contradance"

Mark Rudman (guest editor), *TriQuarterly*: "*Giovanni, would you*"

Michael Schmidt, *PNReview*: "Centuries," "Four Rivers and the Pennsy Yards"

Jon Thompson, *Free Verse*: "New York Sonnets" ("Aquarius"; "Green, Yellow, Red"; "A Bridge Beneath")

Rosanna Warren (guest editor), *Ploughshares*: "New York Sonnets" ("The Battle of Anghiari")

To Katharine Burns of Greater Boston, I owe one very good line, among other kindnesses.

Contradance

CENTURIES

Keats stared at coiled hair—John
Milton's—and felt blood
drenching his face, as later
he felt the same hot
acknowledgment before a
Greek cup, all life flocking there
at full-bodied ease.

And yes, there is that great one's
unsurpassable
doing, then the javelin
thrown anyway, the
uncoiling lunge off the block
before that whisper over
the shoulder, before

they toss up the white flag at
the finish. And yet
beyond sparking hair, just past
all those burstings in
the young man, an opening
onto fields, blown curtains onto
standing bending weeds

and the wind out of blending
spaces, of what we

call the centuries and then
fall still before—that:
it coming from where, and we
weaponless, the forehead cool,
unthought of. The whole

of that already there yet still coming.

in memory, Thom Gunn

DAWN RENGA

El aire de la almena　—San Juan de la Cruz

Mist from the mountain
unraveling, or is it
the mountain that tears

　　　Where lightning scattered the loons
　　　river steams up into day

He of the Cross, hid
in his bright darkness, lay
stroking wind-washed hair

　　　Under the fan of cedars
　　　when the Lover struck his neck

He mentioned also
a battlement, the wind there,
but no place was safe

　　　Beheaded with all others
　　　who suffered through to union

Hold the affliction
given, perceived by no one,
until you can see

all the rock ledges at once,
all the climbers, swift seasons

and it is the earth
growing suddenly before
a broad sky crumbling

earth headless and giving birth
to itself, warm wind steady

CANTICLE OF THE WINEPRESS

A chasm opened. Through Massachusetts day
two-thousand-three it was Berlin, not the braying
pre-war strut and wedding-feast beer foam
but nineteen forty-eight's dead-drum

expanses; not succulent
vegetables heaped in the stalls of Schöneberg,
nor spring through Karl August Platz, but the dragged
claw through every wall's rent.

Between two blonde bimbos into noon's lull
I slowed among rubble,

and that mute pair felt real, their forearms
warm along mine, a tawny tiny wheat
rippling them. Yet their eyes were tight
crayon crosses, on forms
smooth as a dress-store dummy's,
side-falls flouncing their shoulders—
bleached by the hedge-fund years
or screen stars from my childhood baked barmy.

A hatter hunkered, pounding
velvet that he pulled and pinned around
egg shapes. Up to his shins
piled the cuttings, strewing lemon, soft greens,
violet and raspberry from his shears,
and though I tried to break free, his wares
fascinated my zombies

                    and in the year that it was
the underskin of stone shone through, as dust
shines through dust after days of fire and the pulse
of its mica wavelength chills:
Gloucester Point lay winking flat east,

yet if the hatter who only seemed busy
was still mad, then what was I?
Berries staining their splints, woozy
tricolor peppers trucked to the Kreuzberg, frenzies
of cut blooms in sunny gusts—these compressed
across the mesh in his vats,

then smoothed and drying in those mothy helmets
still guzzling the grape's pulpy drool,
siphoning attention through their wicks, all
thickly into the briared foliage that forgets.

I knew that the unfortunate bear up
or rage loose, while the oblivious regroup
around the necessary as their shaken good—
dew bunches along a scythe's oiled blade—
but what I knew stood impotent. Already
what those dolls wanted saturated my power,
troughed scarlet gargling the brain's cauliflower
into solar stillness, the blast of it steady.

And just so I was squeezed into the winefat,
where though it crushed me I too was that shoulder,
in the drench of its raiment and wool one long scour
swiping to loom clean through two-way light,

with one motion my sloshing step in that place
through all my blood.
                Thus the price of release,

        for there was none now with me,
for I had rolled dumb through my anger and trampled out
a fury that I recked not, the stain of it
soaking my shirt. And to whom shall I report?
        For I had gone among a throng
yet of the people there was none with me.

Flowers and Birds of the Four Seasons
with Sun and Moon
films of matter upon matter
compactly, intriguingly, and

came Chernobyl.
And through
the sleep of one witness a clod
at terrible
velocity passed her. Screamed.
We call it matter, dubbing it
stuff—all which fosters surprise when wraths
burst neutrally, keenly, from it.
And the momes rath

outgrabe.
        Our race
is that
woman of means with middling
talent, the nice but pushy pupil,
who came to
aging Lizst—he, reduced
to taking such people.

This time she was
halting in the runs, slowly repeating.
He stood at gaze

gripping his arm,
then slammed
both fists down. *Enough! Don't you
know who I am?*

SOCIETY OF FRIENDS

Oak benches in the meetinghouse parked swept wings in tight formation,
 strategic bombers mothballed in the Mohave, around the aisle left clear for
 George Fox's dreams of quakes and volcanoes.

What had flown into itself was still arriving, its long touch-down narrowing
 the shimmering far tarmac.

Quakers and No-Nuke grayhairs, with cloud piling tremorless midday, faced
 two *hibakusha* waiting to testify through their bespectacled translator.

Hiroshima's Khota Kiya stood at attention in solar tie to debrief headquarters,
 the coal red on his tongue after some sixty years. *I walk, can talk, work. My
 government wish strike Article Nine. I come here your country thousands miles.
 Useworduvmouth! I can walk, talk.* He was my age.

In what world if not this one has he already scaled the barrier dune,
 his mount slipping nine times but achieving the crest with his mutilated,
 shining tenth form? Here, it flashed once, going in.

That night in the grass, the unmown cosmos, October fireflies left their lights on
 for the last time, low far lanterns.

GIOVANNI, WOULD YOU . . .

Giovanni, would you
see me
alle cinque, Chiesa Nuova?
To talk. I have to.

Overworked teacher
and weary
paterfamilias,
shy would-be searcher . . .

we had been guests
at a friend's.
Now I sat where the Corso
Vittorio thrusts
widest, the smooth steps ripple
away from the barney church
and pigeons breathe
stertorously
among bronze hours, and watched a protest
march gather hoarsely

in the oblong square,
the blind
gypped by the state led there
by the blind to roar
through their bull horns
and step off
in waveringly good order.
A cart of melons

got sideswiped by
a leathery
motorcyclist, who doffed
helmet and drew up to the splatter
and paid for three more than he had smashed.
The old man twittered.

A waif on crutches
swung and
swung through the mess with whoops
kicking swatches
of rind, a crone
cackling
back of him filched one up
to taste, alone. . . .

Then it was those
I'd remarked
other evenings, now
among strangers, haze
from the late rush
acridly
holding the heat, and the whole
air of it threshing slowly and greatly
up through
that vast parlor, none of us
explicitly
invited, over our criss-cross
making for the blue ceiling
with a sound never quite spoken out
and a fragrance
obscurely of the occasion,
of all those there met—

so I sat for three hours,
and the desperate man never showed,
who in his rare delicacy
had dispatched
all that company, all
those beings to me—

their half- or no greeting,
or straight on,
aiming at something we sensed,
moving, or waiting—

my appointment
was with them,
and now, these years since, with
this deep content.

TO THE ONE WHO STOLE MY BOX OF TOOLS

The way a man's knees lie one over the other
when he sleeps on his side, the knob of one in the valley
hollowed just shy of the other—that is the way the legs
on those calipers that you now own, the forged ones
with their full-moon hinge, will nestle into each other
if you have any sense in disposing them in their lift-out tray.
The whole kit is now *lift-out*. You have forcibly
reminded me of that: life is no possession
but an inherence, and the Italian *martello*
retains its self-presence no matter your hand. And may it
fall just shy of the nail head into the face of your work
with the same reminder to you. I speak you no malediction.
It behaved that way also with me. Nor do I propose
to haunt you with my own presence, as Chief Seattle
advised us that the spirits of his sons and daughters
would stand beside us in our factories and offices,
and lie alongside us in our beds, and mingle with us
at our weddings and funerals. The crystals of my sweat
in the knobbly cherry-handled screwdriver will merge
into your sweat as themselves, their two poisons
of sodium and chlorine neutralized in a balance
pungently, immemorially impersonal.
They shall arrive, my impromptu colleague in labor,
in the same way that parallel universes ooze forth
from the black scalding cauldron of hyperspace
and the souls in them, and the souls in ours, engage
in sleepless commerce although we sleep, go out
on missions we know with tasks we very well know
and tools that have become second-nature, although still

16

we sleep, waking more tired, a bit sore from the carry
and mute transposition. May you slowly learn to haul these facts.
What you heisted greets you with the completed faces
of the desert hermits and communards after they had
stolen themselves from the Nile towns, and Rome, and Greater Greece
in the imperial diaspora of anchored ground, and enters
your hand as they passed tabooed boundaries, complete
in demeanor of usefulness: this universe to that universe,
trekking to reinstallation in a mud cottage
as fresh as its own face—having seen through everything
and thus speaking only to the bulls-eye, utile
and melodious, discourse going compactly and tartly
and mind entire from middle heart to middle heart
and gut to gut. Wherever you came from, they came from
behind and beside you, ready for new use, so that
courtiers at Rome traveled the seas to use them.
That is the kind of face looking up at you
out of the bed of that dinged box, and when you sleep
it is their piercing and serene cheerfulness
that rests alongside your uneasiness. Life is not a thing
that we have, it is being seeking employment. Do you not wake
at times gifted with the shudder that an instrument
has made its way into your presence, waiting for you
to recognize yourself as the quondam user and itself
as something that will continue? It colonizes your rooms
with citizens of presence, completed inhabitants
of process. They, now, will be able to enlist you.
That which you are in your short-breathed shapelessness
they will employ to make into another shape
and then migrate into finer grasps. Those men and women
of the Egyptian badlands seem to us maniacs
in flight from body, family, and taxation, who only
wished to serve with flesh more completely what flesh
honed and oiled can serve beyond even athletes and legionnaires

and temple prostitutes: maximally tooled.
You have chosen the path of separation, like Nietzsche,
who feared toads and frogs and loathed swamps and the mire
yet raided the tool kit of Sophokles. When Vaughan counseled
Run for the mire! he wanted the all-out, not the tormented.
What you got will get you for the getting: what any of us takes
was meant to attend to us. Plotinus said it was only fitting
that Providence reach every being and that its job be
to leave no single one of them neglected. So, too, will it
look after you. And among its means henceforth will be
the Japanese pull-saw unforgiving in its draw, the ibis-headed
tack hammer that must land like Baryshnikov, and
the nested hex wrenches that fold into themselves like banked
organ pipes seen small, from down the length of the nave,
just before the organist lays on Bach or Lizst
or wild Jehan Alain from the pedals and manuals.

CLUB W.

What books did sly
Wittgenstein
take to his hut in Norway,
if any?

Already there,
firs swayed near and far, and silk
water tongues blurred.

Sway and slide: slaughter the ox of each certainty,
thus to read better the spines of branching questions,
their solitudes and swerves.

Not *Whom does the Graal serve?* but *What makes you ill?*

I brought *Parzival*
to a clatch of lifers, the knight who was granted a second chance,
having failed to put the question.
The impossible
connection
returns if, in harrowed simplicity,
you can go to hell.

Why is the entrance
chamber
yellow, twenty feet tall,
and lit with amber?
Cameras scan for the growth of small trees, for fjords
that could hide a man.

The Roman Questions,
why could they not stanch the red
ooze of high station?

One in tennis shoes asked why
his friend squats fetus-like in the crunch
of a Dumpster these twenty years.
Now that's a good one!

The untrashed questions
hover in laughter or chair-creaking quiet,
as compactions downward:
If we are glints blown from the dark, are we not extinguished?
But is not anguish a guide, fire my cleansing bath?
These the flints to strike with.

The one in tennis shoes sat opposite
the studious and probing one in rimless glasses.
Their friendship threw a swaying rope bridge
between gaming and the serious.
Once it was strung, my task was to stay on it.
Here inside, while remaining someone from the outside.
Serious penance requires its games.

By staying inside, monks face the thought of death,
protected from the outside's scattering of that thought.

Why do they empty our pockets of mere paper, and box our shoes?

Over work stations and intersections, and buttoning
the collars on stilted lamps in parking lots: if mist drifts
through their cones night-long, where are the walls?

Wittgenstein's father brained him and his four brothers
with ice and contradiction,
pushing three of them toward suicide,
those weathers gusting the curtains and folding screens.
Iron and steel made that daddy,
Mahler and Brahms came to that great house.
Does wealth rust the body?
Paul pounded a Steinway. Ludwig designed
door handles for a brave new bone-bare house in Wien,
not locks but knobs and the faceplates.
Where spiked north rained and misted, did he
throw away the key?
Did its arc wink and glint steadily?
A dictionary for spelling and pronunciation, this
he made for the contrary children he schooled briefly
after leaving philosophy.
And, wild one day, he brained one.
Sought to enter an order,
the abbot steering him away. *Unter*
alle diese Dinge,
beneath it all,
where lay the fruitful question?
A hut in Bergen does not beg questions
but rests them between summers and north,
seasons and orientations.

The men had read or had not read the assigned bits from Wolfram.
Straight off, a wiry man bolted abruptly, arms clasping his chest.
The closed book of that face they had opened many times.
Their care carried the rest of that hour
and carries their valedictions:
They are taking away our basketball,

they are cutting our time in the library, you gotta come back.
And the guy with glasses, who studied the story and asked all them questions,
is in here on a frame-up. He didn't kill no one.
The classes, too, soon were taken away.
Slap as they folded their chairs:
PROP. OF LIFERS CLUB

Wolfram's cub knight like Śākyamuni Buddha
was sequestered as a youth and so blurted raw questions.
Thus his trainer yelled, *Don't sweat the small stuff!*
Keep your eyes and ears open but your mouth shut.
Wittgenstein climbed backwards down the ladder of questions
to those primers and then toward a monk's cell,
forestalled both times, and finally, unraveled, found himself
greeted as a god on the railway platform in Cambridge.
Only these cons, minus the one who did not do it,
performed a slaughter and then were left,
mostly without means, to come up to the actual
emotions in that situation and not turn away.
To become, not combatants or philosophers
but alert inhabitants of many-times rehearsed pre-formance
which lets performance arrive at its first-ever, inside-out second run.
Just enough food and exercise, but ever *la composition.*
In the third movement of Mahler's ninth,
pursuing a tone shorn of vibrato, Bernstein wrote in capitals:
ALLES KALT.

That was fifteen years ago, one-fifth of a lifespan.
If the chivalric simpleton on his leash were here, by now his mother
would have grown testicles and turned grandfather.
And would have walked him beneath the surveillance lenses
saying *Up there, to the right,* but not pointing.
And walls? He would leave those to inference,

22

though under the gooseneck lamps in the parking lots
he would mutter proverbs:
the lights are always left on in the house of the dead.

Say one had never before
seen cumulus spiring snowily far off. And there
it looms: the first
and the last
and leaning without end.
Which is rarest, sight or the seen?
On Ludwig's grave pitches a tiny ladder,
as if in the vision of the martyred Perpetua
or earlier in the Neolithic pits.
Rains veil the middle distance
so that the plainly foremost enters into full evidence,
the drenched grits no one studies.
Where are the children
going,
and where have the right names of things
already gone?
The pot boils so that
ointment can seek illness,
even the spills working
into our reaching.
Where but
here? And never the same,
into it, searching.

AVEDON IN HIS LAST DAYS . . .

Avedon in his last days
remembered Jean Renoir in his last days
playing host to a large Sunday banquet,
the portraitist a newcomer to that fold
abashed and pretending gaily to make talk

while craftily sidling to the bathroom
and from there furtively toward the door
signaling thanks to his host, who bulked up
into the tubular walker which still carried him
and cornered the escapee:
                    What matters,
dear Richard, is the look exchanged over the table
while all my other friends are gab-gabbling away,
our recognition, is that not so dear Richard!

The Lord of Generosity enters from his own house
into yours across a garden at midsummer,
and it becomes clear that you were not at home
even to yourself, the great meeting
forestalled one more time—water
brimming the beaker, jam
and a fresh loaf broken in the brown crock:
at home in alteration, they shimmer to rest
steadily cadencing over their last ground,
their incessant giving and taking
slipping the latch on the door to a cool evening
into which neither the owner nor his guests
nor his dearest one have ever looked.

24

NEW YORK SONNETS

THE BATTLE OF ANGHIARI

Boarding the local at midtown, all seats taken,
he worked his way through the car with firm lean arm
from his black tee-shirt pulling him down the high
stainless-steel handrail. Through that forest of bodies
flashed his teeth: in spasms his lips would pull back
and his eyes rage, then calm. Neat, perhaps thirty,
the self-enclosure of the others a gapped curtain
for his tic, the racket of the express
for a steeled moment harmonizing it.
Then a seat, and he sank into his paperback novel.
Leonardo caught him in sketches, head
twisting in red chalk over one shoulder yelling
some command, the neck's tendons wired, the carry
of that voice drowned by the long cacophony

and thus unheard anyway by those left standing,
the din still in their ears, they not yet home.

TO MELVILLE WITH PRY-BAR

Your liberal captain saw at last, but late.
You took Pip, Billy, and Bartleby, aphasics,
to hell; took Milton to sea for metaphysics;
sailed rebel from the clan but not the state.
Why have I dreamed you in this day of vandals
climbing to your loft at the Custom House
in the Battery, if not to prove the use
of endurance? Hanging there Dante's worn sandals.

Rocking a rotting stump out I work the rest
of the answer loose: sudden easings of tension
with the intractable; the fluted and belled
shape of the hidden as it massively crests
and yields; and patience, patience with dimension
in the shadowy beryl of the sliding swell.

AQUARIUS

Dusk still cascaded down the stone scarp, over
warmly lit plate glass where two couples dined.
The vast, dispersed agitation of the thing
our shared life is for a breath parted and held
itself away, those pairs encased silently
glad and engrossed, intake's miniature—
Upper East Seventies, the late push homeward—
when a tall man carrying two satchels, neither
manager nor professor, stopped and bent
wearily from the waist, setting them down,
then found himself continuing to topple,
both fists striking. And tried to stand, but could not.
A cargo truck halted between us, shaking,
rumbling, then jerking into gear. And he was gone.

GREEN, YELLOW, RED

A London banker to one of ours: *An intellectual
breakthrough! The poor are honest. Who would have guessed?*
Old Tortoise piping from his shelter even as
Baudelaire's dandy strolls with him on a leash.
Crossing Third, late sun inflaming the cliff
for ten blocks, dip and rise humping amber tail lights—
I stop half way, the rest of the pack pushing on

strung like the gawking throng along Thames bank
just below Turner's lookout toward Parliament
where it torched up in yellow, orange, and soot,
the marble bridge where it stoops to the other side
fire-lit and molten. And I have this moment
before these massed headlights lunge out in their scrimmage—
have it with those who linger in the breach.

I HEAR YOU CALLING

Upturned, her face demanded that *mine* be truthful—
gambit reversed. The porch of an uptown church
framed her cowl, towering wreckage by a tower
whose door hung bolted. From some ripe depth
came her hoarse blessing, then the aperture
shut once more, creases near her eyes as deltas
fanning to gulfs across a mind, a world.
Alms, alma, trauma, tremendum, lorn, learn: what book
binds their leaves? Not the boulevardier's album
of glancing encounters. Daughter of disasters
curling wholly inward, nestle thy babe,
your rotting shawl hanging lank, let the hot wind
billow it soprano, though not for thee
such releases just yet, not here, not now.

PHILOSOPHIA, EAST 65TH STREET

Heidegger's Greeks over against Cassirer
and Jung's memoir, Jaspers, Arendt, and Weil—
a teenager breaking into the seas of
philosophy, or the gleam of philosophy,
I was my village: twenty-five hundred with Poles
and Polish exiles, Hungarians from the failed rising

sponsored in three homes, and the hemlock forest
behind the immigrant college infusing all this
with speckled shade and plausibility,
like the pines in the country fair hung here in varnish
among spurred panoramas—an engineer
stiffing the Russias, ribbons through the mazurkas
advancing in ranks through gloom past a winding stair.
Kosciuszko! Metaphysics, the defeat tradition.

A BRIDGE BENEATH

Midtown slabs of improbability
vaulting on lucre, one-way panels arguing
that their stuff leaps over mere materials
into some other substance and scale—their loft
through mauve dusk and the gleams sunk in their grids
held my rube neck bent back. But second sight
had that steel glass turn watery. Divination
sank a blue yawn of fathoms over a bridge
suspended in murk, folklore arch for a troll's den
glooming beneath with Curtis Lemay's bulbed head.
We actually had those people. At the railing
a little crowd gazed down, then Dorothy Day
turned from one of her homeless, approaching me:
Yes—did you want to speak with one of us?

INWOOD HILL

Hosts off to work, the abbey museum still shut
on its citadel, I trailed up ruptured paving
toward the river gorge. A half-circle
of benches had been stripped, spongy plank-ends
from a few grooves, the black and rust uprights
a unison of treble and bass clefs

tilting backward. Everywhere, vines and brambles:
my own Connecticut River *disturbed landscape.*
The semi-same, the aborted correspondence,
will shuck its own seed! Out of uncloistered ruin
a freighter toils alone through mist up Hudson,
cooling contrail zippering the beyond,
Sufi dribbling up-dune en route to the gathering.

THE PROJECT

Manhattan Project: Dad smelted sheaths for The Thing.
His part in all that has not yet settled in me—
straightforward in the living of professional
momentum and its unknowns, over against
the fact and fate of first use. His gift to me,
however, from near the piers one June night
at a cut-out along the West Side after the war,
met simplest need with his mute fellowship—
going down from the car to the mile-wide river, unzipping,
and letting fly together, grinning at vastness,
we framed a simple stand-off, shielded by
the eternal barrier, toward his open-hearths:
alchemical pre-gold streaming from us into
wave-chop set alight by Jersey burning.

CHILDREN'S ZOO

The plunge of paradise birds through lianas, hothouse
vapor and drag sliced by young human cries—
Mister Charles Darwin was an amateur
slow and laborious to the firing line,
but as tenacious as Grant, so the shareholders
built this: a bird tower around a fish folly,
where a titan bottom feeder paces with barbels

in S-curves before the ecstatic face
of a two-year old, her jumps rigid and squeally,
arms out at her sides in Granddad's camera.
With reverse English, this place turns us in and away
from the accelerating extinctions. But already
the water is inside. Life, it is late
to court you this way, aye, *ars brevis est.*

VITRINE

A locksmith's window: pastel orbs and steel collars,
corroded shanks, brass casings for the cams,
these knobs cropped from a harvest of the unhinged
and house-wrecked, these the no-more-at-grips,
roll and untwist in the pasture of themselves,
nestling to shiver the grass of graspable law.
Gilded or silvered solitaries or dumbbells,
a dormitory sprawl from the night of nights
and the feast of feasts, they wait for Belshazar's
great morning to be hung from the silk nets
of ebbing torchlight riot. Films of exhaust
sequester me from huddled voices, tables
populated by shining goblets, sheets whispering
down a blind-drawn bed, cubicles of tart truth.

THE WEB IN CENTRAL PARK

Sangay Choden, twenty-some, sits in harness
to a frame loom from Bhutan in the entry passage
of the Rubin Museum, her hips the yoke for that silk.
At breaks she anchors it like a horse to its post.
The monstrous gods here are meant to scare you quick-time
into reality. Thus, six, astray in the Park,

I faced three toughs converging down a rise
carved by Olmsted from his love for England. And Dickens
was their weaver: mute cut-outs against the light,
they would have done for me in that first chapter.
But I reached the street—an untested C.O., let off
by the motorcyclist who chased me down a Rome alley,
and clear of the clubs at the napalm shipping point:
to tense the weave while walking away, that too is a calling.

ANFITEATRO FLAVIANO

Riots in Latvia, Lithuania,
Greece, Bulgaria, Hungary, Iceland awash,
from Lehman Brothers, the two-handed headless engine
by the doors, windows, cracks in the walls, false paper.
A swipe of my finger along the pink granite
of this bank yields the same grime that settled
on the gilded giallo antico parapet
back of the cheap seats in Rome, where roars entered space.
Decibel dream, stone gleam, the dream dreamed by many.
Four stories down in the Colosseum one gallery
parks a horse-drawn fire rig with rawhide buckets.
A photo from 1900 shows a boy
hunkered over his spinning top at arena
zero, above him the ranks of void arches.

THE CHRYSLER BUILDING, MET LIFE, TRUMP TOWER

This skyline staggers the gapped teeth of Saturn
chawing his own children: we put him there
and them here, vapor and blood streaming through
his cranium at sunset, the same phantasm
perpetually reenacted. Sunrise, though, that

rude bud of flux unsoldering itself
from the cold rim, bulging through lower heaven
unfiltered—for mere mesh it atomizes—
raw—for no oven cooks primordial fire—
and crashing the levees of social bond and story
terribilis et fascinans it insists,
as illness the herald leaving a man kicked open
to illumination shatters the wall of one being:
acetylene, access, ardor. Killing, and kind.

LIBER STUDIORUM

As in the book of sketches by Mallord Turner,
from the left, blood in a serpent torrent, its gush
valley wide, the fate it bounces churning
out of sight yet glinting elation—thus
boogieing red the horse of the Second Seal
shatters its neon outline and just so
this is. The long presage of dread whelms past
chill to the source while rhinos thin out to foam,
dolphins arcing out of it, pink faceting
its torn waves
                      while two rooms away the purling
of someone making water, and May's night air
cooling the sill, squirrels a gray fuzz over
thistle spill from the feeder:
                            balances born
from nothing short of keenest effort given
utterly over at the crests of cycles,
incapacity at last carving destiny
from the dead hero's side as all look away,
dawn's flush threading drenched grasses: full flow
ungraspable, your standing surge dark bronze.

HAMMONASSETT, CONNECTICUT

A big boat splutters distinctly though I fail to spot her.
But I need not scout far for the source of presence
to join with it: the deck, the horned bronze clews,
taffrail and stainless steel wheel. At thirty-three
I knew the naming of the parts, at sixty-six
I go with the sinuous wave line on a craft
for an entire minute. At seventy-six
I'll soak it through the layers of marine varnish
to the mahogany.
        This kind of hearing
is staged by a lens of air that bends sound
back and down, reflecting laughter and wrangling
over miles while twenty feet off voices stay muffled.
Long Island bluffs talcum a denim ribbon
under wide cirrus. Slowly the beach empties
though a matron in blue silk and two combed boys
set up folding chairs, families gather,
pastor and groom from one side, bride from behind,
the white train soundless across sand, her three
children and his two escorting her.
They are all volunteering a second time.
White shirttail loose over the man's hips, the starry
blanket of earth-sea that Zeus wove for Hera,
all his crazed opposites cinched tight and shining.
Homily floats in, but the state is younger
than this bond. The two boys pass triangles
of white paper from baskets, and butterflies
stagger up, zigging toward dune grass, wavering

back down and resting. In the book I brought with us
sixteen townships send noblewomen to Elis
to stitch up clashes and then weave a robe
for Hera, thus peace. At eighty-six I'll have sat
with my own ruptures long enough to hear
white water burbling up cracks through black rock.
The bride smiles within a sober face
for the cameras, then unsmiles. The groom consoles
a girl who bungled her part. His hindered brother
brays then swings off in a half crouch: these are
what the dance movements in Beethoven's quartets
pulse out and usher away. And because they are here
this couple has the goods, they have made majesty
do andante through rock powder. The cyan parlor
of afternoon stays satiny for two hours—
men fishing from jetties through the ceremony
wait on that other Paleolithic pledge,
hunt under wave, over moor, through thicket, still
on picquet in their monumental pause.
And still feeling official, the boys fold chairs
and stack them, cirrus cotton-candying high fires.
Again, the wide empty stretch, staying as if
some unseen power had zoned it clear out of
delicacy, or respect for the chances, or wariness
of menace. Empty . . . but then something massing
back of the light pulls it taut, an everywhere
nation, the thing that growls that it must be loved
and obeyed, its low consistent tantrum having
oldsters parked in wheelchairs over sand
fearfully smiling trying to recall what might have
set it off, and with it the wreck of something
enormous and briefly valuable, its crumbling

going on while nothing they see corresponds to it.
The nothing I see.
                              See. Yet I did: bridal thighs
in copper maturity under blue eels
tattooed across her dimpled sacrum—that badge
studs a mute vaunt across the fathomless rumble
thrumming out of nowhere.
                              At ninety-six
everything I do will signal to everything
I cannot do across a bridge of haze
at the northern rim of the Canyon, no separation
and all alive.
                              Leaving we come on a pair
of black swallowtails pressed flat against tussocks,
ants on their bemedalled tuxes, their glide
past exhaustion. Blues on the trailing fans
recede irrevocably among rows
of stuttering sunspot orange, their entranced
vesper showering firework sulfur through gold.

A VETERAN

At four on the street he broke
from his mother, overcome by an impulse to throw himself
under the big truck.

That girl in the news, the one
born with the twisted face, what will she do? His hand
floated, seeking some zone.

Loner who survived 'Nam,
who framed up an apartment in exchange for the right to live there,
fine prints in every room—

gay carpenter who did not
delay but was misdiagnosed, now approached just as I must
the power, not to submit
but to lose then relocate
his fit within the entire array. Which pools and presents,
leaving nothing out.

The Pequot war loops mist
through his riverbank backyard, leaving me to let in
that mad link or resist—
slow whiteout that numbs. Lately he'd cut at his limbs,
how many other attempts?
But now he was really leaving, sixty-nine, mets pressing in,
from the cells a greatness preempts

even the old destroyers.
Walking trails to the river, he startled a young buck

staggering up through shivers
hobbling to flee, the gullet
ripped like the flank, a red smear struggling among laurels,
shifting there, then quiet,

the black nose flaring. *Such, such*
dignity! he whispered from that encounter into
the might of the too much

and the uncannily mirrored.
Yet the mauled animal came to keep a wound open,
not worshipped or admired.

No playing at adventure—
this when fantasts, gulling schemers, and circus
spew their manufacture,
dispersing the will to push back
or even to fight one's way somehow into the clear.
That he felt himself a wreck
more keenly before dying
took him out on the stream at maximum, not like the stoked
king boats but as fraying
fine fabric.
          That year chimeras
rose in Monterey Bay, photographs from robot
undersea cameras
off Point Sur trolling the grave
of the giant reconnaissance dirigible USN *Macon*
lost in storm, 'thirty-five,
spotlights scanning the four
biplane Sparrowhawk fighters strewn from the vast belly,
wings planing into the floor
of tiding muck, and the girders
of the hull's acre-wide rings spilling across debris fields.

Mortuary ardors—
surveillance is the child
of reconnaissance, but *connaissance* the mother
of a weightless gold,
even for the sorry
assessor of a drone-blasted wedding and a mountain
beheaded for coal, one story—

casting back I watch silt
go past the lights and silently tuft itself over
one world, victimage and guilt
unacknowledged under shared time and space, and toy
with that impossibility,
dropping bolts in the ooze, the plumes of it climbing
a sudden front, a sulfurous
brain in free dilation.
                              Don't you know what this means?
booming at Zecharias
past seven burning eyes,
Neither by force nor fiat, but by my fire-wind mind!—
that amperage at gaze
over mountains, seas, ranging through the universe—

thus wounds kept open as ways
for the unknowing, as once
I halted down a gorge when a stag sprang across it
and its head and rack in the trance
of seeing caught where the body
had transited, and its eyes turned to carbuncles
nailing the distance, steady.

DUCHESS

Angling through stalls at a gas station, old Mary
in slurred elegance asked for passage to a truck stop,
Do you think that you would find it possible. The chartreuse duffel
half my weight was possible. But no truck stop for hours.

    The calm in this *domina* stilled me.

No scanning as on that regional out of Milano,
risen sun through a coach of Nigerian women,
leers and disdain over wheel sound smoothing resolves to work
the streets of Florence. Unable to move, they probed freely.

    Captive to a condition, she was on the loose.

Her laugh showed the uppers half gone, she who had done
ward rounds, still ghosting the face of young Ruzicka
counting Iraq's dead until killed, Marla sporting red cowl,
Mary a black beret, both traipsing unprotected, unscheduled.

    Body the same, but not the name on the chart.

As self-givers sink through ignited sky, self-undoers scrawl sparks.
What they are may not be you, although it shadows
your stretch of the wall and veers wide through cloud chambers.

    Bumbling thumbling in the heart's hollow.

Prince Andrew spun his mount where she stood, and a couple
stranded her in their new home, plates warm and heaped.

The same name as my mortgage agent, they were playing with me.
The laws of cooling bodies hold for both defeat and victory,
winning and losing are not explained by them.
Our torture subcontractors she linked to surgeons, insurance.

Blames and evades, but does not mock her own vices.

She had owned houses. She had entertained. She had counted napkins.
And saw names migrate from death certificates to closing papers.
I have not enjoyed Earrrlll Grrrey for some time now, lorgnette pinky lifting.
At market pug Silenuses hinged open on figurines of the gods. *Socrates!*
bubbled Alcibiades. Gapped grin, then shy gaze sweeping a heart locket.

The mission of a seed is to immolate itself for a strange glory.

I get four hours sleep, scan the truckers for the least obnoxious, then make my move.
Rounded backs at the counter, lit signboard into night, the Stop.
Like us she is a quadrumane fetus fitted with the sex of Cleopatra
and a thief's chromed cunning, all shrouding the will to respectability
in the land of the twice-mortgaged bed.

By its hotter sheath fluttered, the flame's heart spires and sways.

Not ours the cycles of revolt and reaction, Second Republic and Third Empire,
holdovers scrambling for new perches. Not ours the moldy and patient
Colonel Chabert as he resurrects himself from official death in battle only
to shed every claim. Not yet ours such alternating current, nor the third arm
with which Chabert dug his way from the mass grave into snow.

To solicit attention while eluding focus: last-round defense.

The lawyer who in amazement followed Chabert's greasy greatcoat
was willing to lose twenty-five louis to watch *the greatest actor of his generation.*
Years after photographing the bronze of Shinran Shonin in New York,
brought intact from Hiroshima, I saw down one fold of his robe
the half-soldered heads of six screws, a discrete X.

He trekked the roads of the islands, his staff rust-chartreuse.

As, cloaked against February, a monk tunnels hoarfrost in Edo time.
Wanderer, your mount's sidewall eyes let you bob squinty and absorbed,
while Mary shrouds warpage in faded muslins and reeks.
Nod, and you bore through wilds not yours but hers: a wood
of marvels, handouts, and loneliness, the forestry of ice and courage.

BOOK OF SERENITY

dressing on the 14th-century compendium of koans, Japan

They said he had gone to Harvard,
troll by the yawning compactor at the town dump,
working the green toggle, his face disdainful
of conditions, or himself, it was not clear.
The bottle as his other toggle, that was clear.
One Saturday he was gone.
Weeks later on a bench near the pharmacy
he shines in white shirt, shorts, and cap
enthroned on its red planks, smoking in the sun,
Waiting for my lithium.
Slurred speech and swiveling gaze have a rest home now,
I was losing things in the apartment. You're retired too, a'nt you?
One eyelid high, one hooded, in a lawn sprinkler's sweep.
You taught poetry at MIT? My brother went there.
They had gone to the same prep school. So he knows the feeder lines to the Ivies
and the Infinite Corridor with its frosted glass doors to Materials Science
and what the family mastered, all those other toggles.
The wine god at dawn near the city gates
ordered a pair of stooped elders to caper and jig.
A determined quirk can run anyone. So where, then,
strewn among the trash of the dance, are the alternatives?
Fayan said of Old Jiao, *That man puts on no show,*
he's like the eight-legged pot set in sand, no wobble anywhere.
The black strap from his back pack
shusses the white shoulder down his puffiness

under a stubbled crag.

I served in Germany, began reading again, and after a breakdown

came back to Wesleyan for two years and studied the poets in German.

When Fayan had asked Jiao,

Did you come by boat or land? Jiao said, *By boat,*

and Fayan asked, *Where is the boat?* And Jiao said, *The boat is on the river.*

And smaller than a mountain. Outside the meditation hall

Larry Rosenberg suddenly had faced me,

his abandoned tenure at Harvard part of his talk that night,

and I thanked him for the backstop which that gave in retrospect

to my own crazy exit through the transom of learning.

Taking me by the shoulders he said, *There's a saying by Lin-chi*

about the honorable man of no rank.

Another Saturday man approaches the red bench to pay court.

We nod and I give way, but facing old Ozzie I recite,

Herr, es ist Zeit: der Sommer war so gross,

and he lifts his smoke high: *That's Rilke!*

It is year six for our floodlit *Lager* in Cuba.

Along Euphrates the legions spit out obscenities just north of defeat.

Then in its little white bag the medicine arrives.

Lin-chi rose in front of them all and said,

The honorable man of no rank

is always coming and going through the doors of your face, just look!

And a monk stepped up: *What is the honorable man of no rank?*

And Lin-chi grabbed him by the shoulders and held him.

FIRE

The placard among clippings as on a dorm door
LACK OF CHARISMA CAN BE FATAL gave onto
one eye glazed with much seeing, the other glinting welcome.
He eighty-five, twenty less on my side, we flanked an oak effigy
of Hans Jäggerstädter at the age he was beheaded, young farmer and father,
Ja to the way and *Nein* to the state.
Walls soared with the blue in the cut-out *Fall of Icarus* by old Matisse.
Old Jesuit had said *Yes* to the young queer thinning into virus
and so inherited the Andean poncho
spreading its wheat and rust bars between our rockers,
had said *No* with home-made jellied gasoline to the impressment
that sucked up my generation, said *Maybe*
to the young cons and resisters he had taught with his brother
in the Big House. *The real one of us all. And yes, the man in the memoir,*
we got him out to Stringfellow's house on Block Island.
Ashes down that sea cliff to wrinkled continuous burning.
I said foolish things, forgetting I was there.
He said *Yes, Yes,* to weavings climbing that blue,
Ecuador, Guatemala, El Salvador in yarns orange and ochre, *So many stories.*
Which are not mine. What we breathed together was smoke
dispersed by five-hundred-pounders behind
three smears slanting over my desk, the sky oily,
a man in shirtsleeves crouching near a girl,
it might be in Central Park after she has lost something,
his arm around her. That was in the first year
which by then had six replicas: the explosion inches out rallantando
with a rushing sound stilled into steady quiet
for that delegated *abū* is sober, halting on the way, great is the power of the way
though the whoosh rolls over them, its hot knuckle flung by the old projectors

44

onto wobbly screens, our teachers wiggling the tripods,
numbers in black rings flicking backward to cross-haired zero
with hairs squirming to stay in place then ripping upward
leaving arctic marzipan, the reel whirring, no one moving.

Mighty the draw of the way, no one else along your stretch of it
regardless of the shouting and crying, your ears full of that
only because each has been sucked or dragged
proceeding singly athwart the draft in the concerto
where the chorus draws hungrily on each voice,
Norman Forster throwing aside his babe at the last moment
as benzine shimmer luminesced, curling from his crown.

     Incontinent though contained:
the belling, the blurring, the omnivorous today—
blossoming as-is from the fizz of its own basis
     until counter and aflame—

in Genesis as in the *Iliad*, fire, and in Acts, fire
the tar of feeling in the *Iliad* wrath, and in Acts guilt—
the way inhales each one and sets him alight
past our consolations, as in this man's tribute to loner Gerard Hopkins:
a glimpse of the chamberlain in those posthumous rooms
emptying bins of papers onto the orange hearth—

sun that neither rises nor sets but unsolders
its own vitals, giving over *ad maiorem gloriam*.

PAPYRUS FRAGMENT EGERTON 2

A little crowd, and the question came from him walking:
he spoke of a thing *shut within its place* . . .
set there below invisibly . . . *its heaviness*
past measuring . . .

like Ives's *Unanswered Question*, all a-hang,
haze and mass of anti-matter, or of anti-question.

For the record says they were puzzled.
And that his next act was to stand on Jordan bank
extending his right hand, filling it,
sower to the river.

The verb for what happened next has gone downstream.
Before them, though, it became *present* and *put forth*
oodles of fruit whether figs, oranges, or olives
a gap now hides, and whether
the sudden orchard rooted, trunks browing water,
or bobbed and stilted away. But their joy,
that is recorded.

A question had gone unanswered. Or else that answered it,
everything enormous met with the lightest touch,
non sequitur.

Indeed it does not follow:
to cloud, swimming unfloored depth
apeiron the root of rebels.

Or it does, though as an iron check to explosion
sensing what pins one gazeless region to the other.

If it all floated away they must have followed
clamoring: a *Winter's Tale*, the statue swaying, breathing.
Sower. River. Fruit. And under them,
the ponder press of the enclosed thing, of the enciphered
megaton seed.

1618

She must have stood in the crowd,
his word entering her.
The painter's Negro girl,
in Philip the Fourth's Spain
a slave, is his outcast choice
for the Emmaus road house. Already
in Brazil the Jesuits
have built their first sugar mill.

Cleopas and the other
flank Yeshua at table
tucked in a corner viewed through
the kitchen partition. They frame him
but do not see the reality.
Facing us, she turns her
head at the sound of that voice,
not fully, only half way:

left hand on a wine jug,
with the other she steadies herself
against the counter. It is
stop-motion, and it is
stop-breath: when he'll break bread
of course they will see, and then
he will get up and leave.
But now the knowledge is hers.

And she's ours, with floating shadow
that sags free, and another
that hugs her outline. Velasquez
that year in *Old Woman Frying Eggs*
showcased brass and ceramic
with the same up-front offering,
forcing his patrons to notice
his skill for the cash bait it was.

Which means convertible value.
Two account books in her bodice,
the present thus nests in a mystery
that unavoidably
we know about even if
we seem not to. And here
it hangs, the change-point, yet here
too glows magnified clutter.

Still life is life stilled for
the feast, the old rites, their
silent incorporation
of loud union. These hammered
brass bowls are not for sale,
this raffia basket bulging
from the wall, fluffing out linen
half-clean, has asked more of life.

No, they start to weigh more:
garlic heaves white lead
to a poise, its spotlit crinoline
strews a shroud minus body.

An inverted pitcher broods
black pools. Together these vessels
lag on this side of being
seen for what they are,

still sprawling as salvage: Alberti
a century and a half before
with pontoons and winches at Nemi
failed to raise the party-barge
of Caligula, yet he pulled planks
from its breakup: lead sheet, bronze cleats,
ribs of larch. Ball-peened knowledge
drags the eye in, shy of fire—

shy only a while, however:
there in the mortar lies
powdery what propelled
Catherine Earnshaw and me,
there too my ambition
to extract and hold what the pestle
scrapes out sickeningly
into solution. And so,

bronze mortar, I have known
not only your heft but also
your mash abyss, and yet
the heating, the cooling and standing,
I walk with them in my mind
only so far, their future
stands just here yet dark and
brawled matter yearns for completion.

The resurrection body
pushes past these thick boards
and clattering pots into heat
with the woman, with evil, with worn
stuff of all kinds, those unfaced
quintessences. The durable
crowds out through the final
cook-off, past gleam, past seeing.

FROM THE FACTORY IN WOLFSBURG

There is no beauty in New England like that of the boats—George Oppen.
There is no beauty like that of weapons—David Jones,
who tested that proposition.
An itch is at work between them.

Both things as old as Phoenician trade, as knapped flint.
A B&B Anchor-etched chisel m/m 25 drop-forged
seats itself in oak coifed with a brass noose
to accept the tapping hammer.
I have left one corner of its leading edge snapped off,
that nick bringing the near-eternity of the tool
within range of ourselves paint-slashed for the axe.

Our millennia with the animals, dangers scaled
to the mana of breath and eyes, we traded for imponderables.

It was the later 'sixties, night flaring along the Bay
as we drove Jake Ander of the Kingston Trio
to San Francisco's airport. The People's Car, the Bug
preserving the seed-form of Hitler's prototype,
slowly lost speed, not responding to the pedal.
I got it into the breakdown lane, and we coasted to zero.
Jake and his Martin guitar were due in Chicago
so we lifted the rear engine hood, clicked a flashlight, and stared.
Hailing a trucker and clasping
the matte-black Bette Davis shape of his Martin,
Jake was swallowed by the cab.
Then headlights behind us: another Beetle,

a blond strider with black bag.
Haff you a deefficulty? The eyes acetylene blue.
I comb frawm ze factory in Wolfsburg. Fhat year iss it?
A 'sixty-three. *Ach, zat vass a bad year for ze fuel pump.*
Jhoost a minute. The provision from his kit of the part,
the surgery, then a short-sleeved clink-chunk twist-tighten.
No charge, ziss vun iss on ze factory!
A wave-like salute on folding himself in, and he pulled away.
Had Jake stayed he would have crooned his refrain:
Noooo, that didn't happen!

It happened. Its boon, though, is that of the iron wolf,
apt, even fabulous. Thus its bane is the iron teat.

Among her visions from the 1930s, Christiana Morgan
saw the birth of a child with clubs for arms, claws for feet,
and four eyes gazing in the four directions. A cosmic thing.
Nothing to do with Miss Morgan, Jung assured his seminar.
It was suckled by an iron wolf, like the Latin twins.
Ezekiel's four-headed seraphs, the seven-eyed Lamb of ire
in John's jamboree of revenge: the itch at work.
Little clubs for smashing things, the buds of something age-long.
She wept and passed by, as any of us might.

I want our incident along the Bay to stay clear of this.
Which it can if I simply pick up and resume.

Saying that it happened by saying that it didn't happen.
Clearing out with my instrument and making my connection.
Marveling and going home.

But feral thought demands the lie that greases it.

The phrases in that thought are long, their tails loop around other thoughts.
The unsaying of such thinking writes a long amendment.

That unsaying requires unthinking the manifest frames.
Demands oak-handled blood-flecked tools. Which we left at home.
It will take us a long time to get home.

Not the weapon, the boat: immersing in conflict, to steer
mind and heart through it and, leaving, to leave no dent.

Down the iron nipple a glisten that quenches no thirst,
neither firelight nor starlight, moonily gathers
where opposing powers hang through each other's potencies.

Love, slow to judge. Then the rathe oil of action.

INCOMINGS

On the curve of the airfoil
yet as gloss deep in that metal
sun smear drags illumination
firmly across wrinkles, rivers,
grace of the drillers on the rigs,
of jungles pressed into black pools
by rock masses: over that hazed
and riveted convex mirror
for the sky's face the newswoman
Politkovskaya saw nausea,
poison working in from tea
served to her on the Rostov flight,
she, called to Beslan to dicker
for Chechens who had sequestered
eleven hundred children, all
at school. The Russian Army, foiled
in dealing, wanted her away.
Her blood tests from Rostov vanished
on the flight back to Moscow, trace
elements trackless. In two years
her elevator cage became
the box into which the last test
poured red and maculate over
her spilled groceries, the emptied
pistol dropped among all the finds
she could not live without, what her
stove worked to render. For she served
only what she craved, unwrapped from

crinkly darkness or mined from want,
truth factored by no one, the thing
down the middle whole, quivering.
Berrigan and Zinn, surrogates
for those sending the planes, Zinn
a bombardier in his young youth,
soon to be hoodwinked and strong-armed
by their own missioners, flew to
Hanoi to retrieve downed fliers
and, sirens then, dove with children
into tunnels under a night's
tall tonnage. The children: with them
at last under our bomber fleet
and asking beyond speech for shield
over child and self, Schild to Schuld
among the long-shelled with the heart's
German of pre-prayer, the fore-Greek
of ur-Sanskrit, *satyam ucur*
as sunned puddle in a footprint
even in a black shaken hole,
act of truth. That one only thing.
Into the hand of the woman,
on the buds unroofed there in that
soft colander, as radiation
shooting beyond any half-life,
spirit descends: the aeons-long
climb-down of high fire presses in
to the levels of the oil,
uranium, cesium, down
all the lattices in the metals,
the grids and slicks of conjunction,
so that from the knit bone we can
resurrect now in body what

already it pods as seed, break
open around its inherent
vitality to be clustered
past the surrender point: just here
the bride thou art. Those carrying
Bosch's blindfolded, severed head
in the vanguard of his parade
have them all, fore aft and both sides,
openly watch the commissioned
killings, the mountainings of loot,
for in this place visibility
is immunity, while unread
stays the long-loved misgrasped symbol
of risen body, steadily
fed by vineyards and fields, the fruits
into which fire spears without let
slowly and ever-present, keen friend
and interpreter, with its news.

FOUR RIVERS AND THE PENNSY YARDS

Laid out on cowpaths
                muck then mustard brick
Pittsburgh, East Pittsburgh, the South Hills coil and trail
sinewy. By the 'forties stick by stick
plank stairs and sawtooth roofs still clambered up shale

framing the incline, barges, staggered bridges
on Ohio, Monongahela, Allegheny.
Rawtooth, fresh soot each morning on their edges.
Bessemers lioned in my sleep, orange, runny.

I came back at sixteen, a scout for Yale
sizing me up. And stayed one more whole day,
Father insisting I choose my own hotel,
have breakfast over the newspaper, play

at being my own man in the city. Toward
evening I walked the Ohio bank near the tracks
my engineer grandfather worked, the Pennsy Yards,
stilled, stopped, all that tonnage as if in wax—

where I stand again and think of his pranks but remember
what I knew not then, strikes put down by Hayes
and McKinley, three hundred freight cars burned, lumber
and creosote smoking like the mills for days.

He joined the union. Even a freight engineer
in those days was a captain though working-class,
and mother's legend for me—from twisting fear
that ruin would get us, dropping her back in that mass—

was that he scabbed yet left bags of groceries
on union family porches at Christmas, Easter,
and Thanksgiving. Cunning and swift, the disease
of not seeing while climbing, each onset faster.

The Hungarian worker's family I loved in boyhood,
and later Poles, Czechs, and the American blacks
I knew in the boonies, still composed an étude
for repeated practice, no informed attacks

both hands on a keyboard into the harmonics
of earth, its substrate *work* going down for worth,
Slavic faces at pause in heat's tectonics
rippled at the bay of an open-hearth.

Father built those furnaces. Built sure,
then the 'fifties sealed Truman's coldness in steel
with a hot button. Slowly I've built toward a cure
for that witchy underchill, its case-hardened real,

so I love marshes best, their percolating
interdrifts of seethe and settlement, oozes
to life's beginning—slowly reinstating
my passion for metal too because it fuses

the pouring with the hard, as of one mind.
And in fact under the rust of those Yards
an artesian river bores, the fourth, black, blind,
for not seeing is seeing too. In hard

Bush Two's era, decades after the mills
came down, I stand within my youth's odd body
sensing as through bird's legs to where it thrills,
that unshown roar, the unseizable fourth, steady

cold in that clean force cleaving rock. And watch
an empty hopper cut loose by a switcher
drift through its reduced maze. The scope, the reach
of what has been stifled here trembles out richer

for rumbling the flesh of fifty years up through my feet
out to the exurbs, through this iron to the mounds
and tailings among farms. Neither hope nor defeat
but earth is what that sluicing sounds.

CONTRADANCE

The frame for a large poster reproduction
we stowed in the car, then entered the pub, the waitress
asking about your Reiki book, she too a
practitioner. The journalistic poem
cannot afford to inquire into its status
because it can aspire to be no more
than it is. But the diagrams in there
show sunlight between the opposed palms yarning
to skeins, balling to an accordion,
then stringing out genetically in mitosis
otherwise unseen. Our dishes served,
her hands beside them conjured the auto wreck
that broke the bones in her feet, arms, and face,
intact black Irish lissomness describing
how her mother gave her Reiki through the casts.

Sealing the dancer into the big frame
I cracked one corner of the glass, a slash
barely visible across her earth floor.
The enlarged notations of the researcher
who did the watercolor stream around
Etruscan motion, the chiton and skirt
filmy white, its red rings gauzing her skin
which he remarks is *rather clearer than
that of the men* painted in the same tomb,
Solo le bande tre Rossa, only
her three forearm bracelets red: technical
notations for the lithographer

who would never see the fresco. Thin lines
of each limb through camisole and skirt, arm
arching above her raised face, one foot toeing
outward and down in a low dandled kick.
Fingering the faint green slice across that glass
I realized I never would have guessed
the mended breakage in that girl's face though
I knew too she could not have taken in
the radiance from it as she spoke. We are not
allowed to observe our own holiness.

OUT OF STRIFE, PEACE: . . .

Out of strife, peace:

to the man fearful
because
of the not-done at the ends
of doing; to all

that a girl hugged
to herself
through lone years rather than
being dragged
from what she alone
knew
to accomplish; to sheer
sound in its keen
sallyings from
a scarlet
beaked invisible throat
beyond roofed home—

peace: for

to compose with
blocks and
masses of sound—as the shelf
of ice full width

tilts off, or as
a swell
gathers at midsea tasting
its future fizz

and crash: as Schubert
slides
tectonically across
forest and covert
in the wind's motions
and a
freight train, stuttering, clinks
with the Venetian's
chittering strings
as they
move out into long lanes
of beginnings:

      this, when at last
the whole
weight in you moves yet you know
you are its least

executant;
that you
are with, and shall be through
your own event

carried; and that
such thrust
comes from the one who hears

the whole, whose great
hurry across
the score's
unblotted sprinkle means
that like a face

the solid entire
radiance
is what he reads, and now
releases, sure

of the long push
behind
being, his own with the rest,
their stillness, their rush.

for John Matthias on his 60th birthday

VENICE'S LAST . . .

Venice's last
treasurer
disrobed one night and bathed
but did not rest.

The treasurer
of Venice
who came last had prepared
an accounting, sure of the next step,
unlike
the Chinese counselor
who carefully steeped his tea on rising,
not knowing
whether he would survive until evening—

he was at it,
warming
his pot, when from behind
he was beheaded.

      The last treasurer
of Venice
took nothing, practicing
divestiture
as he rowed out
making for the Lagoon, raised canvas
and cleanly slit the moon's track

for where?
What do we mean when we point
Adriatic

gropingly, thumb
blueing?
He had committed no crime.
We have no home.

His oars were not
muffled,
the sail was mauve and burnt orange,
maps have no feet.

      Venice's last
went—
joy is a world anchored
rocking, one must set out for it
when the time and the accounts
have settled that between themselves,
the final
manager reading that flag
where sun dissolves

the remote lion
and with it
the puckery domes, banner
bright and then gone.

ACROSS AND THROUGH— . . .

Across and through—
the Pont
massively convex,
night yellowly

sodium-pinned,
my resolve
was to track slowly down
the time flank, wound
the thigh of passage
arched at
convergence, and regain
one room's edge.

Palms waxen
in lit fogs, the laboratories lofting names, toxins
regulated by bronze entablatures at lean,
and the dilated intersections,
projecting from cornices, of demons
with passions I would have lived
had I not aimed
across and still through.
Past the enslaved

trinkets behind
hard sheens,
carpet sogging the drains.
Past the red hand

hung from mock gold.
No longer
did I know where to stick in
my knife. Ferruled

moldings, achievements
simplified
by black blur, hung along
the web of pavements—
the chance to strike multiplied—
and I was the assassin
who had lost track of his victim
but yearned with fresh hope for the little
sun at the rim
of his own threshold.
Myself
when I got there would be
the man I killed—

and the sun there
to us both
would be being, its there
inhering, fire
that only is.
Lovely
this odd killing, most lovely
through it to seize

my odd brother,
quit of departure and destination,
given to neither.

R. M. R.

I didn't get off at Raron
by the Rhone, from the green local,
his stone inscription backing the church there, needle through
the stilled commotion of the peaks.
Not there, in fact, his meanings.
Didn't see Chateau Muzot
with his outlook on St. Anne's vineyard chapel
except from the coach as it wakes
through creakings

to cut what the river has not cut,
the world letting welded iron
slice through it, tilting the long cars
through the bankbooks of the eras.
I didn't detrain at Sion (Sierre)
but his ticket, too, lunged beyond it—

he took a compartment on the *beau monde*'s
space shot, for Austria was his Florence:
a lukewarm exile, not quite
Dante's, not yet Milosz's, flung him
among the metropoles, his Italy being the whole.
When a good table in villa or hotel
or house on a pasture hit him
with *that Paris feeling*, he could feel, at last, well.

The nobility aimed their last defiles through the mass
as sealed trains of the gone, yet these got him
to his sunny perch under the high ice,

still moonily ornery:
railway cuts, canted multilanes,
the windowpane ice-crystal stems
of airport runways, the clogged
aortas back of hydroelectric dams,
these web each other, they have leagued
against his itinerary
as a city man near the cow-runs near the vines.
In a passport photo his eyes
bulge quizzically over woolen lapels,
a loden coat for Mount Purgatorio,
its goat-chewed switchback slopes
for the speedy who know there is little time,
even through long mornings, the pen coming to grips.

Most of the counts by then,
the duchesses, princesses, landgraves,
had purchased their tickets—*We must be
on our way to oblivion*—
turning their studies under the deep eaves
over to Chinese Orpheus,
his moustache a downward bracket to Hades,
the high ascenders in his script
teasing the lines above them for egress,
a bolt into daylight—

he too poked through into alarums
and put on the uniform.
A military snapshot presents an occluded
Mandarin, files under his arm
from the Arsenal, aware
soon of the convulsion's
waste, the evaded

recognitions beneath every shared
intimacy, and how his forward position
had set him with no more protection

than a quilted morning coat
at a lion-legged desk under the big windows,
his exposed salient flush
with the arrival tracks, soot
from the terminal mushrooming under his *Schreibtisch*.

Neither cleverness nor fluency
abiding in the long glare from those windows,
his German no longer quite German under their vacancy
and that a strange boon, the cracks in it
extending space to us, and beyond us
to the accelerating human,
for better connections between the hells
are mere bitterness where the shucked temples
sit back, forgotten women
evoking one unforgotten woman.

Absent? The law ever present *der Gott* unforgotten woman.

Even the planets are destinations
in the hands, now, of the traveling kind.
Yet still, behind rage, fear; behind fear, stations
of betrayed trust, hard little hand—
the forearm-polished plane of the worktable
stills and compacts these, even the projectiles,
to the almost capable:
beneath its oiled walnut a black draft out of the *Bahnhof*
billows, the express down there gliding out,
its guidance neither in signal tower

nor the station master's cap and coat,
for curls of that plume, her hair, trail the power
to call her up, the tonnage easing by half
as it gains speed out of the yard:
rocking momentum, her recovered aim something heard
through clickings among the points
                              and this he draws
intent only that it rise—

this in report after report of the action

for there, at the moment of maximal pull the terrific
tug shears and neither express nor girl
arrives, consensus pitying the smashed effort
yet there I'll descend:
                    Orphic
God the incalculable hidden in us has been led
thus out of us and pressed
into the orange on pines beside winter roads
burned there by salt, into the dirt
down the steep treeless rings above reservoirs,
in grease streaking roadbed ballast
corkscrewing into the mountain, in weedy spill
above trenches—
                    sunny peace mounding all those scars.

in memory, Sidonie Cassirer-Lederer

73

BOOK OF THE DEAD? WE HAVE NO BOOK OF THE DEAD

I have done no evil . . . , I have not caused pain . . . ,
I have caused no weeping . . . , I have not brought suffering
to anyone . . . , I have not copulated, I have not misbehaved.

Not that powers themselves fade. Their grip on us lessens.
The final Apollo has been caulked and polished, the last
Aphrodite sanded, oiled, and catalogued.
                                        It is time.
Unrolling it down the pasture like a banquet tablecloth,
helpers to the balloonist spread his red means
slashed with puce and white like the puffed thighs of Swiss
halberdiers at the Vatican, then they holler.
Igniting the latent core of actuality,
torching the anthropomorphism that passes for it,
he aims a tubular frame into the vast yoke.
Billows undulate around its bass hissing and swell.
In a mauve frock coat from his great-grandfather's day,
even though he is a sifter of fissionables
in the era of miasmas, he pats a gray top hat, silver buttons.
Pats his waist-high son, and checks the wicker pannier.
His appearance says, *No, I am not capable of this.*
No, I have nothing to do with any of it,
no, not this technē. Yet he will sail jetting flame
in momentary dragonings up through puffed pleats.
        It has begun already: they stirruped him into the basket
and slackened the anchoring guy ropes. The schools
of philosophy were once ardent gangs competitive
about the task: how to live. Caps wave, hankies.
They worked out the protocols, tensed the cords, slipped them,

the separation they celebrate gives a master to freedom.
　　Such nuptials of possibility with discipline
rely on a harmonic of tricks. Usually the flame
wobbles, destroying. Gilda Larocca, taken in Florence
in 'forty-four while running the short-wave, escaped to Milan
with retinas scorched by the torturer's lights. She had said,
No, I didn't know that. No. No. She could still type,
and so two patents, for ink that lovers could daub on rose petals
and a couch that became a coffin, passed through her machine.
A weightless stationery for amor in hell's hour
and a seat you take with you into weightlessness: the *No*
begins to slide onto wilting surfaces.
　　For Old Top Hat, the basket stays basket. His frock coat
is no mesmeric bon-bon of the escape artist.
His drift is not away, but across the live and furry
in a mirror of the dive. He wagers the dimensions,
up as down, as free-fall, and pollen big as towns,
a seeing particle among the particles, roar then silence.
Metaphysician, and how not watch him?
　　　　　　　　　　　　　　Craning my neck back,
again I see boys drop snowballs down the face of Strasbourg's
cathedral, who, if interrogated would say, *No, we didn't do that,*
while what attacked was not their toys, it was the air:
a stinging tartness with molecular teeth, supplements
from Trinity, the Reich, Poland, Japan, Brazil, Bikini
through one lifespan. Whiteness muffled the whole cliff
though one might still hear, in all the languages, *No, we didn't,*
no, not us. Couples at the portal under the gallery
gawked up at dots enlarging then ducked among the layered
saints and queens.
　　　　　　　And here I am watching a maestro:
he leans from the rim coiling in a rope, receding
as slowly as Rev. Tanimoto in Hiroshima's park
rowing his loads away from the flames with a bamboo pole.

The fire works for him this time. They are safe. He is diving.
Through his ropes the buzz of the lived plane resolves to a hum,
pattern and heaviness apart for an interval.
From the third outrider of an unnumbered sun, lifting
as diving—this, too, the human may arrange and patent
if it has sat to its task, lived its dual nature,
for though sandbag conscience will lift with it, gray ballast,
all has been readied by sandy Egyptian sagacity
to deny complicity. For it is human to say,
No, I have never sinned, no, not, bare-faced to the powers.

VIOLIN

With all pasts and futures harboring in this present
then all, happiness and unhappiness, is a choice
if only because I have agreed to build here. Yet even
the most daring choose happiness alone, and thinking
will never get me through this, and feeling loiters in it—
only Great Harbor floats all of it, fresh, waiting.
Following descriptions of the North Pyramid at Dashur,
the Red Pyramid stripped of its red sandstone facing,
then photographs from recent expedition reports,
I found no speculations about precisely why
this pivotal structure slopes at forty-three degrees,
a matter of moment, perhaps or perhaps not, yet
I saw sand shelving along the base of the west face,
a ripply ledge smoothing along remnant facing
and blending with it—the same as on Plum Island,
barrier beach for piping plover and pale-belled sand shrubs
dropping its steep bevel sucked at for miles by surf,
the rolling sound momently sinking away in it,
its high edge fronting dune grass nervy against sun.
No Joseph among us to build granaries, no Jonah
to ironize destruction, no Jacob to hammer choice.
One third through the mere sixty years which saw the great
pyramids rise, this one, with the lowest inclination
at forty-three degrees, *cautious* some say to forestall
shiftings which skewed the vitals of the Bent Pyramid
somewhat earlier and three quarters of a mile off,
was the first achieved prototype. A slope which has me sense
greater mass and area than it commands. A discovery

about proportion and it may be an application
of lore no one yet has been able to read from the record.
This time the architect lifted the burial chamber
higher inside the mass—the squared cone of sunlight—
and for the first time aligned the coffin east-west
with tomb temple and the sun's track. Its capstone
pyramidion was of the same red sandstone,
not the gilded white stone or granite of later practice.
The entire casing bulged slightly outward much like
the faint entasis on a Greek column, though not
meant for Greek good looks, but rather for what would stand.
Altering the slope's angle rise by rise with
cord and peg, masons jesting with the overseer:
this innovation in masonry was not imitated.
Senefru, who enjoyed people, calling his staff *Dear Friend,*
the only king known for doing so, presided over
erection of the Bent and the Red pyramids, as well as
two others at Meidum and Seila, the start on Egypt's
Manhattan Project, four solar fusion battery casings
for his charged body, at three locations. He was buried
in this one if its hurried completion is any evidence.
Osiris's theology by then nosed ahead of the astral one.
An east-west journey at night with the sun in that god's boat.
Setting out through river reeds, their silken forgivingness.
On one side, barrier dunes thrusting up into solar acetylene
which tracks with me along their apex, while on the other
vast drenchings sink into the low slope. Four fiberglass
fishing poles shoot lines off into surf, their necks
bent studiously, their shanks in tubes rammed into sand,
their armchair owner dozing under a blue towel.
Four nylon zings of tackle as if sounding unison.
They baked loaves for him in the reliefs. He himself ran
a race in the Heb-Sed ceremony, as did his fathers,

all in renewal of their powers, his predecessor loping
hugely across the slab which seals a shaft at Meidum.
Though no tides any longer moisten the stones, those tunnels
smell of the sea. The burial of full-scale ships
began under his son Khufu near the vast piles at Giza.
My ears ring with a cricket-like susurrus that comes from years
of holding taut line out into the oncoming rush.
A certain age renders further ambition supernumerary,
my buried boats need no more cult. For all the forces
at play in this wide theater, its spaciousness declares
a propertyless state. May I now take up
the violin that nearly came to me at age ten,
my maternal uncle's gift? Brought ceremoniously
on a special visit, yet it went back with him, the fact of it
raising an outsize grief in my mother for herself, perhaps.
Or spite at my father, who stood back, declining to intervene:
our pentimento for strings, over with on the downbeat.
Rest in peace and the mystery, with the silent thing in its case.
Or may I pursue this engineering further?—Surrogate
for the womanly body of that fiddle gone downstream.
Yet they were building spirit reservoirs, surge tanks
for seam voltage, soul-welding solar granaries, and one architect
had been chief priest. The hand tracking shadow at Dashur
from rod to rod for the foundation's first course of stones
may have held a lamp for priests in the last chamber
as rare privilege—for their ordained invocations
tested by many sequencings, happiness on alert
through ordeals, the chances awful and the aim real.
I woke with the sand grains of his destiny alive
across my maroon blanket, mustard golden spores
thrown over him by the king, a gift of land to that
Dear Friend. Deir of the geometries. His eye through the pile,
its red slope, the Forty-Three: design stabilizes the *mana*

of earth lofted into fire's force and held there,
steadies the dangerous changes. Guards against them
even before the end, so that a fine instrument
recharged and tuned during the royal run but at last
taken away may morph to mastery in some other walk
by another sea. May turn—mangled god—mischance into the path.
For this I sing: Deir of the triangle with plumb line
portable and pendulous in his eye's mind intending
this for the powers, the king and people, the realms
interlocking, past calamities, through dynasties dangling
in the shaky cycles of order.
                                    I took from his case the still shiny
stream-bottom varnish of the thing and chin-clasped it
per his instruction, and before setting it back in the inky
blue plush drew one long wavery whine
from the G string, pushing up slowly with the bow.
Delight broke from his face. The dark closure not yet
having come across hers, she parted her lips, eyebrows
arching expectantly. Labored, nursed, caressed, that sound
could go on past the end of its own curve, such was
its Pythagorean hint even in my raw hand,
animal miracle among the ratios.
Next morning it was gone. This then sing:
that were I to walk that sand's bandwidth between desert
and facing stone, I would tread neither the waste
nor the monument, but one string stretched like the dune's world
behind my barrier beach, scrub and wiry foliage
nestled minutely into pockets of the in-between
and giving ear steadfastly to immensity.
That close to forty-three degrees is where the G-string
lands a bow's tilt, as a pro will testify.
That even the smudge across her happiness, and the murderous
touch of *creatura*, and the inept weight of fate,

dissolve where the soul burns and melts, where tone
and overtone release each other, and if all stabilized things vanish
in the furnace, truing the line and lighting the chant
give love to the fire. An immense fragrance rose
from the dyed velvet of the case, the sealed wood,
strings, rosin, fogged black saddle of the chin cup,
the untreated inner wood of the curved body,
the equine substance of the glue, the fluted pegs,
ivory nut to tauten the pale sheaf of horsetail,
and a man's sweat and breath, when he opened these to me.
I have not imagined myself long in the burial chamber,
neither as carver nor priest, and only for a brief spell as builder
scanning the ceiling slab for telltale cracks. A vast
aroma lifted from that case among the bright faces.

Flowers and Birds of the Four Seasons / with Sun and Moon names a Japanese painting on silk.

Dorothy Day's greeting in "A Bridge Beneath" was reported by Robert Coles.

"R.M.R." draws indirectly on the bittersweet task of sorting papers for editing, including letters from Rilke, that came to my late colleague Sidonie Cassirer from her mother-in-law Eva Cassirer.